The three Kids who killed a Werewolf?

By

D. David Croot

An elegant Introduction…

There was a time when kids were free... Is this not true I ask? I beckon an answer for your mind to give yourself alone. Freedom, innocuous innocence. Blissful ignorance. Time tested gears of all our hearts and minds cannot for one moment doubt the belief, the internal inclination, that we were all once indeed free in the absolute!

No, no! Do not look to the lovely looking person beside you, all dressed up in their Sunday best i'll bet.

When was the last time you dressed up for the occasion? Wedding or funeral, rarely will you make the effort for any occasion other than those you are morally forced to go to.

Bare this in mind as I converse with you, answer for you and hopefully enlighten all who are around to truly listen. Because listening is such an itchy skill. Always does it seem that somebody wants to interrupt a railing train of thought or usually…change the subject to something they know more about or are more interested in.

But today folks the question before us, is universal and will affect all of our hearts. Also, it may be the hardest facet of life to really reckon with oneself and confront the inner demons and think for yourself in all areas of life. But this is what I need you to undertake. This sojourn will not be pretty, you may even hate yourself afterwards and the answer may well not be all too clear.

There can be no if's and but's, we may very well be setting down golden precedent here ladies and gentlemen and this is no small feat. May I remind you that we shall be a part of history here, regardless of the verdict.

It is taken as a given that you are all different and have arrived from and drive through all walks of life to be where you are here today. Correct? Of course it is. We are all different yet bound by the same immutable laws of man. There's plenty of room for opinion, in fact it is my own postulation that all news today is opinion and this helps nobody. So if you can, when you leave here today and every day afterwards. Avoid news of any kind. It's not good for you, makes it so much harder and far obtuser to make up your own minds when it is most needed.

Again, sadly, much like everything that runs and rifles through the mind this is only my opinion and as such cannot be proven on the dot, scientifically.

Which again I truly believe is one of the only beautiful dimensions to life there is...

I'd like to try a little exercise and thought experiment if you will. Before we start for real and I promise you I will close my mouth, we all need a drink and something to eat but we are not dealing with just one case here. This deals with the core of humanity and you'll be blessed in my favour especially if you remember this salient fact...

...I would like you to cast your mind back to that place in childhood where no wrong could be contemplated let alone debated then forthwith annihilated with the harsh viscous vicissitudes of adult life. For there are comparisons, distinctions between the child and the adult that cannot be

denied. When a baby grows into a man they have always been the same person, have they not? No need to answer I've got plenty more for you to contemplate. The soul, the Phoenix rising from the ashes born again Christian male is not what I am getting at today. I would like to simply state that whatever is, always was, would you not agree ladies and gentlemen...

It certainly felt that way for me when I was a young cherub in all my former glory. I was a right messy one. Look at me now, do we change or do we all become? It's not so easy to answer or even see within oneself, especially upon the verdict of others we do not know. So…let's get to know them together shall we?

Do not worry I shall see it on your face. There shall be a collective grin, a little wink or sudden eye movement that let's me know we are in this together and on the same wave length and only then can we go forth merrily as one…

From your own time as a child, whether it be bathing in the sink when you were at your youngest...First fondles and kisses with the beauties of the class, that one good teacher you had for a month or two. The way you won your first competitive race. The forty-second goal scored in a fifty-three goal season. The way your parents looked at you as if you were the world...Extreme poverty or luxurious wealth. Why I still remember getting full on twenty pence pic n' mix. Twenty pence people! Twenty pence could not even purchase you a five pence piece these days. Yes yes...I will try to stay on track and do my best...

...from your own childhood it's not too hard an endeavour to hop to another. We all had friends right? People we hung out with, yes? Well picture this, eyes closed, eyes open it does not matter. In fact, forget I'm really here at all...

The precious first incident...

…Billy, Johnny and the all round nutter Gary were bored. They felt they'd nailed their youthful examinations and were looking for ways to stir their exciting lives up into a little playful ecstasy.

Football was great, they played each other, swapping roles, taking turns in goal. Heads and volleys. Two versus one and they'd even beaten a rival Gang of Four kids two years their senior by eighteen goals to fifteen.

The game went on forever. The sun had scorched their souls and still they wanted more.

"Yeahs yeah that's right, go back to your mama's cooking."

"Gary, they can't hear us."

"Good, they'd probably beat us up if they

could."

"Judging by the way they played, I doubt they could beat a pine cone. Did you see the way that lanky one ran. All arms and knees at ninety degree angels. Deranged!"

"When he took off I thought he'd never stop. His glasses were so thick…ahh to think we could have been born like that. Losing to kids two years their junior. What losers?"

"What if they'd have beaten us?"

"They should have. No harm no foul I say?"

"And we didn't lose did we. We are the triumphant lot!" Johnny said.

Gary jumping down for the crossbar replied, "Sheesh for one moment it'd be nice if you didn't talk like such a teachers pet"

"Why, it's good to learn."

"We have to listen to her babble all day in class and then you don't shut up." In a rather aristocratic tone of voice, Gary rejoices with, "Aren't we a triumphant lot, yes yes, a triumphant lot we are..." He's almost dancing with himself now.

Billy the more level headed of the group. Laughed and dismissed them both with, "Shut it you plebs," then when he had their attention, "what do we do now? The day's still light. My legs barely hurt at all."

"Poofter!"

"You what?"

"You heard, my legs don't ache one bit. Why I could run a marathon now if I wanted to!"

"Go on then," Johnny replied, "I already feel so triumphant I could sit here all day. But I'd watch you run around this field...say...forty-five times."

"Is that a challenge?"

"You betcha!"

Gary limbers up and tastes the winds breeze upon his tongue.

"Alright then, which one of you chuckle brothers wants to try and beat me then?"

"Nah nah nah, no way, not in a trillion months would I bother with that herculean task."

"What's up teachers's biatch too tired... Hey besides, it's not a race without a competitor."

*"You didn't say race you said marathon **Gary**."*

"What's a marathon without other people running?"

"A helluva challenge," they heckled before bursting into group laughter the only way kids can.

The whole world's before them. Every day is a delectable dream and who wouldn't like defeating opponents two years older than they are.

To put it briefly…Could they be feeling any better than what they did at that moment in time?

They downed the rest of their water and tried to counter the boredom after the high.

"It's nearly the summer holidays."

"We could beat them guys any day of the week."

"I wonder who'll challenge us next? We'll have challengers from all over the county in the summer."

"Nah it'll be the same six or seven kids we always see over and over."

"The whole world's opening up like a volcano to us and you think we'll stick to just this one field and park. We'll go exploring, you'll see"

"Will we. The reason we see only the same six or seven kids is everybody's afraid of the crazies

and the pedofiles that roam the streets"

"I don't see any?"

The gang notes Johnny is overly puzzled.

"He knows Wong Kar Wai and most of asian cinema yet doesn't know what a pederast is?"

"I didn't say that."

"Then what is one then eh?"

"They gather up kids don't they?"

"And do what to em?"

"...Anything they want."

"Like what?"

"Use your imagination."

" I don't want to."

"Why?"

"Why to your why?"

"Why why why shut it you guys and let's move on. The kids aren't scared of the streets, the parents are, not us, no way no how. If one of them came up to me or any of us. I'd kick em right in the balls, no how no way. Then run like I did earlier on with the ball towards the goal. We're outta there, like the wind. Zoom!"

They could hear a disturbing voice calling in the distance...out of the ether...into the ear...

It left them all with a sudden case of the shivers. Well, all but one anyway...

"Sheesh get an Iphone. Who wants to hear that old wino sing?"

"Ohhhhh BIIIIILLLLLLLYYYYYYY time for FOOOOOODDDDD!"

"Kind sir, I shall take your recommendation into consideration. As for now, my ma's calling and I am almightily hungry," replied Johnny.

"Hope she's not too drunk yet."

"I can smell the pish from ere."

"He he he. See you all in a bit, the more she drinks the better her cooking is anyway. She uses more ingredients. Come the end of the month we have nothing in the house but that's a small price to pay for a decent meal every once in a while."

They made their goodbye's and agreed to meet later on after they'd eaten.

"And do what?"

"Who knows, anything's better than hanging around in this crap hole?"

Little did they know, had they stayed in, all would have been fine and dandy and who would ever utter but a golden scented word against them.

Billy ate his slender meal quietly.

Turns out his mother was not as drunk as first thought.

"Guess what sonny-Jim?" She was most bouncy.

"What?"

"How'd you know? Ha ha, got ya! It's not what at all!"

"Did *you*...why are you overly happy today, what's happened? Did you drive your car into an ex-boyfriend again?"

"No, nooo, that was an accident. You believe me don't ya. Me, a violent persons. No way. I drove over him anyway. I went *over* his foot. I'm not stupid enough to drive into him, no matter *what he did to us..."*

"He drank more than you did. He was a bell-end."

"HE HAD MONEY. Anyway, enough of that, I have a job!"

"Oh yeah. How long's this one going to last? I give you four weeks."

"Less of that sultry attitude my boy. I'll last at least five anyway. Could well be two months...well aren't you proud of your mommy?"

"Will we finally have money for something more than noodles in a pot or noodles that are super? Anything that doesn't have to be microwaved or boiled?"

She stumbled a bit, "Well, actually... at first,

we shall be worse off. Benefits pays for most of what you see. But in time if I get a managerial role or maybe even a team leader we'll be able to get you a good hearty meal. Clean up them bones a bit. Maybe even make you smile against your will."

"Maybe a mobile phone? Doesn't have to be an iPhone, but I'd like an iPhone."

"Doubt it, you know how scrapped for cash mommy always is...It's character building. Yes, it builds character to live like this and not have what everybody else has... Look does anybody tease you at school?"

"You know they do. My clothes don't fit and we share the same deodorant. They call me stinky *willy Billy."*

"Well, that's not nice at all but you stand up for yourself don't you?"

"Of-course. There you go then. Make sure you beat em up real good. Right in the face you punch em. Tell em ma said too. That's why I make sure there's plenty of noodles in. You'll grow up big and strong just you wait and see."

Then his mum wavered and paused for a noticeable chunk of time. Her winsome energy had ceased, the day had somehow abruptly conquered her.

She made her way to the settee.

Flicked on the television.

Fell asleep.

Became dead to the world.

Or more importantly, dead to Billy.

The gang were back together!!!

"...My mom's thirty-nine and working at Home-bargains. Any chance you won't take the mick out of me for a least a week or so? I'd probable take several days. Maybe an hour or three."

They all look at one another.

"We might be able to let it slide..."

"If..."

"If what?"

"If you let us make all the snarky comments we can right now." Gary said.

Billy weighs it up in his sad little head... There's an echo of brightness in their sentiment.

"Or at least one comment each and then we can move on. I think it's fairer that way." Johnny added.

"Fairer, what's fair about that, my mom's working at a flaming Home-bargains! Worse the one everybody goes into in town. They'll all know and I'll never hear the end of it! No, there's nothing fair about that."

"We're not gonna stand here, move around or walk along readily excited with witticisms unknown until you can take it Billy and that's a promise."

"They'll be twice as worse if you wait. In fact right now, if we can say what we want to right now, we may even feel sorry enough for you and be able to move on quicker than ever."

"Who knows we might even be able to come up with something awesome to do tonight?" Johnny giggles.

"Do you have an idea?"

"Maybe, who knows, I know..hehehe maybe."

"But they'll be nothin to giggle about if we can't think straight for all of the insults we've got *in out minds ready to burst."*

They were both peeing their pants with dynamite in their brains.

It was not long before Billy relented, "Go on then." Billy was moved by their earnestness and comedic relentlessness. Which went a little like this:

Come on

Come on

Come on come on

Come one

Come on come on come on come on

When he least expected it… another 'come on' would appear.

At the same time, Johnny and Gary gave off the one verdict they knew they shared. It may have been a little harsh but it was only true friendship exemplified as they said, "There there, didn't think you could get any poorer mate."

Did he cry?

Did the earth swallow up and take Billy away?

Did he lash out and attempt to make them appear bloody in the face?

No way, no how… he did what all the good hearted children across the globe did.

"Still got a left foot that'll blow both your skinny legs out the water when it comes to darting down that wing buddy." There was more, "Hey Gary every time you sprint for the ball, you waddle so much I think you're gonna shit yourself and Johnny, Johnny Johnny Johnny, poor ole Johnny stick to playing in net ya chubby cheese eating freak."

Quite simply he insulted them back.

All was well.

All was togetherness.

They broke out into playful fists of haloed laughter.

It brought them closer still.

Johnny's meal and household were no better. He had no mom and his dad berated him and slapped him up real good from time to time were he to make even the slightest cheek inflected remark.

It hurt most when his father reminded him, " You'll never amount to anything. Nobody round here does."

"Just look at me a beer bellied old fool who's worked the same job. Drinks the same meals" holds up his can of Newcastle brown, " and lives the same life on repeat. It's Groundhog Day without any fuckable women around the dining tables."

"Hey dad, I'm eating here."

"Why, why I oughta hit you again. Who is it for you to question your father? My spawn. Your kind. So what? My mantra has become so what! I do my life over every day... if the boss, a real pointless tosser of a human being waltzes over to me and asks me to undertake several little extra duties...I say sure...for a little extra pay...and when his face is surprised at my attitude and he waves disciplinary action in my face...my reply...so what I've been here thirty years and you can't do a thing. I am furniture I am that wall over there...so what...guess what ma boy, they never ask again. And when I retire, not too long now, I'll do the same but even less..."

His dad had good qualities also. The ones really appreciated by kids the world over. Always food in and no matter how late he came home his paps was always there watching the television or drunkenly half asleep dreaming of the most fuckable of women.

That meant something to a lad. Some kids had nothing.

They discuss the many kids in their class. Tearing apart their attributes and in their own contorted way, attempting to understand where they all came from and how they all fit into classroom life...

They all settled on the stinky kid, "Smelly Peterson"

"Does he have a shower, running water a lake to dip his gangrenous toes into?"

"When he said it was his birthday last year, I stole some soap and deodorant for him to use from our bathroom."

"That why you stunk a little more than usual Billy Boy?"

"Fuck you turd."

"Hey, hey, hey I don't remember his smelling any better at all last year, do you?"

"Yeah, don't think he knows how to use it. Musta sat on the soap and put the deodorant in his eyes. Have you seen the jam-jars he's got for *glasses?"*

It was not long before their impromptu bashing turned into a rather creative discussion on what he did indeed actually smell like.

"He smells like un-wiped shit from the anus spread around his body in such a miss mash way that it attacks you from all angles."

That was a hard act to follow.

"No-no, more like garbage recycled with more garbage drenched in the sewers of sadness."

"He looks like, he smells like, stale pee."

Gary, at home, was just ignored. Both parents were alive and some kind've well.

He made his sandwich and headed back out before the shit hit the fan.

He was too loud. He was too quiet. His parents smoked hasish, fucked and were paranoid every time the police cars blue lights popped through their sealed off homely abode.

It was better to be outside where there was nothing but space and time to do as one pleased.

...And, bonus! He swiped the occasional tenner so they could all eat from the local shop.

"Go on then, what was your bright idea pubeless Johnny boy?"

"Do you have pubes, Gary me fiend of a friend?"

"Not really, but I'm the first to use the insult so you can't use it against myself."

"Shut up both of you bald bollocked idiots! All that matters right now is that we do something cool, right?"

"And what might that be?"

Little did they know… Johnny had been edging them ever closer to an endeavour they had never partaken in before.

"Ta-dah!" He revealed.

"What Johnny, I see nothing. No shop. No kids. In fact it's defyingly cold roun here. Don't suppose you wanna lend me your long sleeved goalie top?"

"Then what would I wear, I'd be naked."

"Who cares, I'd be warm and cosy," Gary said triumphantly.

"We didn't even bring a ball to kick against that wall, or this door."

Johnny boy had walked off. The others were yet to follow.

"Give me your top."

"No, why?"

"I'm freezing ere, you know I've got that weird blood pressure thing. Can't keep my temp on the level"

"And that's my problem how?"

"You're full of blubber and it's still sunny out. Come ere!"

"Yeah for about five more minutes and

"And what?"

"Get fucked."

They share and delight in a small game of rough and tumble. Slap and hit, roll and grunt…

"Is that a no then?" Gary ends the debate with.

Johnny hailed at them from above. He'd broken through one pane of glass and flung it for what seemed like miles in the shadowed distance.

"What you doing up there you idiot, you'll fall or worse-"

"What's worse than falling?"

"Being absolutely fine and carrying on being you for the rest of your life."

Gary chortled. Twas a fine jab.

"Hey at least my ma don't work at home bargains where even the tramps can afford to shop."

"We all need to eat."

"I'd rather scavenge along the street floors than have corned beef mixed with horse bollocks from there!"

"Billy my friend, In twenty years you just might."

A cat screened as the dog chased the fading sunlight.

If you cannot insult your friend, I ask you, who else could you bully?

"Come on in to my mansion of an abode fellas. It's mighty fine in here you'll see. Never been freer."

"No way, how about you come down and we'll do something normal like sneak into the movies for free or chuck eggs at old people."

"Yeah chucking eggs at old people always cheers you up."

"Who says I ain't already full of cheer. The air is crisp, I have eaten and I don't know if you've noticed but rather recently I have inherited a mansion of the divine!" He clasped both hands together.

"Is it in the shape of a manky abandoned old factory."

"Yes kind sirs I do believe it is. You coming in or what?"

Creepy calm and desolate was the only way to describe the place. Cobwebs, left behind dreams, sawdust from chewed and eroded wood and concrete blocks. Metal rust filled the air with the aura of a time gone bye. Through the metal shavings, as long as they did not blind thine eye, they were witnessing another world.

One in which they did not have to measure their success by beating older lads or chucking cold eggs at ladies with fat arses pulling polka-dot trolleys behind them. They had found a... utopia?

Billy said:

"I think we should go-

"I think we need a ball-

"I think we should go to the cinema.

Somebodies bound to let us in-"

"What's the matter, scared Billy willy boy?"

"Of course I am. I can't see into that corner over there, the swirling staircase that you just dashed down looks as though it may fall apart at any moment."

"Oh willy boy," Johnny bounces up and down on the middle of the wobbly stairs, "like this…you think I shouldn't be doing things like this?"

"We're not supposed to be here, there's no way we can protect ourselves…If anything falls on us."

"Relax, we're kids! The world'll let us off with anything. I chucked a pen at mr doo-wops head the other day. Do you know what he did?"

Shrugs.

"He gave it right back to me. There are no consequences to childhood. Other than have a good time and let everything else slide."

Once more Johnny came pounding down the stairs, ready to splore?

Gary said:

"Fuck yeah we'll splore!"

Leaving Billy with no choice. It was two against one.

They had no source of light on them, apart from a pre-pre-pre-owned phone they all shared and even that had burnt out of battery earlier in the day.

Each room held something new within its confines.

Little trinkets of metal, tossed away neckwear with the faces scratched off in the middle. An old troll doll. They sleuthed into every crevice of their utopia...

Johnny said:

"Boooooooooooored."

And then

"Let's shake things up shall we..."

They smashed the crumbling walls. Tore apart desks and lived, for a brief while, in the pandemonium of minor mayhem.

They sprinted around delighted within the adrenaline of the newness of new. Not only were they on top of the world but they had a place to return to time and time again. Before it had become a blissful memory they were living on and inside of the tender moment.

…They were a part of something big, grandiose and beyond them all…

Their school results did not matter, what they did with the rest of their lives, was a non-issue…

"Why's that door locked?"

"If we find anything to bodge it open we will."

"Why bother?"

"Anyone want go to the cinema tonight then? This is, like you already said Johnny soooo boring?"

"What can a couple of eleven year olds even see?"

"Marvel."

"Are you crazy. I may not be as clever anybody else in the world but even I'm not that thick as to call explosions and bad dialogue entertainment."

"Dc then?"

"They're both a pile of bloated franchised people pleasing piles of plop."

"You already said that."

"You get my point. I'd rather watch cartoons. Now that's insanity!"

They fall silent for a moment. Was there a rustle behind the seemingly locked door?

Was it the movement of a black cat with green envy eyes that always foreshadows the soon to be downturn turn in our characters fates...

No it was far far far

worse…

"Hey hey, look at this bad-boy!" Johnny had found the most frightening of all toys in existence.

"Ain't that a furby?"

"Just look at its eyes, tis the creepiest thing you've ever looked into. It has no soul but it's trying to take your own."

"MUHUHUHAHAHAHA…"

"Nah, that's nothin, I've seen ya mom in the morning. Reeking of something more than this hideous thing does. Put that shoddy looking thing away will you…"

As ever, the insult de-rails the conversation and lightens the moment.

It were as if, without it, they'd never get along. It was as needed as the air they breathed…

"What do you think they even did here?"

"Not a lot, make shit nobody needed and or wanted, went home and came back the next day and did it again." Gary said.

"Button pressing and lever manoeuvring."

"Let's never grow up."

"That's a stupid sentiment…"

"Why?"

"It's not something we have any control over is it dumb-dumb?"

Billy was beginning to twitch, "If we go home now, we can all stream a movie at my house. Sound good? Would you like any recommendations? I'm into Ozu at the moment. He's the master of the Japanese kitchen sink drama that nobody knows about."

"Thought last week you said Kurosawa was Japan's greatest export?"

"…Yeah…well this weeks Ozu. Life's a learning curve that I'm going to master."

"You really love film don't ya?"

"Movies are life but shorter. In an evening I can take in multiple lifetimes. That's magic!"

"No, Penn and teller's magic. What you watch there's no way you can understand?"

"I take in what I can take in. Might as well start early on?"

"That another YouTube tic tocker, life advice giver?"

"No errr...that one's your mama's"

And to think this guy struggled with multiplication and where to place a comma in class.

The sun, long ago distilled, had now faded and the outside world started to fill with the vagabonds and the retches. The street people who did nothing in the day then suddenly began to rise. Rise out of bushes, sewer systems and trees. Who hummed to themselves about love gone wrong and the birds and the bees. Sitting on park benches waiting for the world to turn, for the clocks to go back, for the viral fantasy inside their head to spin and whirr and grind away at whatever agitated them this morning or twenty years ago...

From up high, in their mansion of desolation, the kids took in the wackiness of the deteriorating day and found a new excitement in the night of the moons luminous arrival.

"Hey maybe dad was right, nobody around here ever does amount to anything much."

"Weird that, we could be so much more the worse off."

"Can they be held to blame for circumstances beyond their control?"

"Is that another one of your ticky tockers? Or was it Ozu?"

"No, just a thought that popped in and rolled off of my tongue is all."

But what was hidden behind the locked door...?

"It's no use exploring the places that are open. We need to experience new frontiers if we are to call ourselves the expeditionists."

"Who said anything about a group name?"

"I did, just now, the expeditionists!"

"I've seen several locked doors or hard to open entrances why bother?"

"We could come back another day?"

"But we never will or other kids might discover what's hidden inside. Tonight is our moment! Tonight we are the expeditionists!"

"It's a big fat no on the group name, but…" Gary holds up a crowbar picked up amidst the confusion of fourteen more furbies, "this might suffice."

"DON'T KILL ME!" Billy shudders.

"Relax, why would I expend my energy on hitting you over the head. We're all poor, there's nothing for us to take from one another."

"I'm just jittery is all, I swear I hear movement emanating from the other side of this door."

"Ohhh emanating, we learnt it today in school you doofus!"

"Well, I was sent out for unsubordination."

"It's insubordination for fool!"

"Guys, guys," Johnny tap taps them both on

whatever he can hold. He's lost in the tunnel vision receding into himself.

"WHAAAAAAT!"

The exit is too far away.

There is no way out.

"THE DOOR'S OPEN!"

The moon shone elastically through the holes in the roof. Reflecting casually off of any non-rusted surface. As time slowed down to no movement at all. A paralysis of the soul, a static moment in time they would never want to repeat.

They are unaware of eternity in a different way now. The surroundings are vicious and lonely now. Their points of view have been scrambled as the door migrates open slowly, a beast reveals himself from the ardour and the toils of time.

It was hard to make out at first.
It moved unlike anything the universe had ever seen.

Danny Croot

Covered in hair, smothered in the moon's glow, its clothes tattered, a blue janitors uniform from the eighties perhaps...

…But they all agreed it was a werewolf…

In the space of half a nasally breath.

"Fucking werewolf!!! It's a fucking werewolf!!!"

"Do we hit it?"

"We should hit it."

"We should run."

"If it doesn't attack us why would we attack it?"

"It's not moving."

Then it lunged at them, caught Gary in its traps, do they leave their friend behind and escape for themselves or do they just stand there hardly alive, mostly frozen?

"GET HIM OFF OF ME, GRAB THE BAR, WHACK HIM. WHACK HIM! WHACK HIS SKULL, DO SOMETHING!"

Easing out of their paralysis the boys move in unison. Billy picks up the crowbar and smashes it over the oddly clothed werewolf. Johnny pushes, shoves and kicks until the grizzly beast lets up his assault on Gary.

Luckily Gary wriggles free to kick the werewolf in the head, "Come ere give me that thing ya poofters."

"It's not moving Gary, let's get the fuck outta here why we can."

"I don't want it following us, might jump from the roof or out of the window, they have the power of regeneration *don't you know?*"

"Doesn't look as though he's regenerating anything to me."

It growls... and... moves a little.

They hit, smash, boot use everything they have left inside of them.

Then sprint away into the relief of the night...

"What the hell was that thing?"

"A werewolf."

"No such thing."

"Then what was it?"

"Does it matter, we're alive and safe and near enough home."

That alienating stillness

was hollow

and

damn near everlasting...

...Solace abound and abundant...

...Fresh was the air they dined upon...

...Wholeheartedly adrenaline filled...

...There was no time like the present where nothing had sunk in...

...where thoughts were merely flashing images of the blood curdling moment...

...As the harsh grey clouds covered the coveted moon they stuffed their bee-bopping hearts back into their youthful chests...

Still out of breath, on the corner, near enough equidistant to where all of their homes resided they relaxed, agreed never to bring it up again and that they'd see each other at school tomorrow.

All would be calm and all would be safe and dandy. Wouldn't it?

Besides

you can't kill a werewolf without a silver bullet!

Can you now?

Sleep

Sleep sleep

Sleep sleep sleep little ones of cherished…virtue…zzzzzzzz

There were no inquires from parents. How could there be? They did not have the power to read minds and were struggling with their own unclassifiable woes.

Ignored or just plain not there, they, the children of our future, disappeared and lived the last week of school as though it were only a temperamental dream or collective nightmare if you will…

Fat Andy had to live with being abused every day... Whereas Billy, Gary and Johnny just had to exist and get on through that one moment in their lives...

...Surely it could not be so hard to forget about, dismiss and move on...

At school they were mere apparitions of themselves. Internally scared witless. Barely had it in them to insult one another.

The teacher had a whoopee cushion hidden on their seat and the pull out whiteboards was rigged with confetti.

The other kids claps manically.

It was all they could do to muster a chortle.

Energy was an enemy, they could not run, even the weaker kids began to chuck crabapples at the once triumphant threesome.

As the week dragged on they became surer and surer they had lost their grounding in this world.

Billy contemplated taking up painting for his anguish, but felt no kin for the Jackson pollock pish he created.

Johnny could feel an unusually ferocious rhythm from within that he just might have to dance out and Gary kept his acerbic tongue whipped upon himself in a self referential introspection that he felt would never leave him alone.

"You wouldn't rat on any of us would you?" Gary the most paranoid of the three said.

"What would I even say, so… umm hey guys- police officer what not, we killed a thing, a werewolf like thing, we're not even sure exists and could you please exonerate us because we feel bad… Why the fuck would I do that Gary? Get your brain together will ya?"

"I know you Billy, you're a pussy and don't you forget it. You'll cave, you'll all cave in the second we're accused."

"Gary we're sitting here playing video games like we do every Thursday night. If you don't wanna play you don't have to. Feel free to fuck off at any time."

"What else is there to do? You got any spray paint left. I could put Billy's name everywhere we usually haunt."

"Are you sure it isn't you who'll crack Gary. You've been mighty fidgety lately?"

"And yet here I am, trying to live a normal life, ready to enter high school after the summer holidays we were all looking forward towards..."

"Gary, now you sound like the teachers pet. What's gotten into you man?"

Gary did not know...it was obviously the horrific event they had been a part of...but life had to go on...the others were okay weren't they?

They lacked originality. They were no longer themselves. Billy, Johnny and Gary, the three amigos, the great and youth-filled musketeers were falling a part at the seams. The stars were no longer within reach, movies held no appeal and video games, well...they were still cool as hell.

It was cold stark reality for them now...

Last day before the six weeks holiday!

Sun glasses were on. A blessed heat emanated around the playground as they lay beneath the shadows of the old oak tree.

The other kids had gotten the message by now. Even fat slobbering Andy felt sorry for them. In fact he even missed their near constant jibes:

-Hey fatty Andy...

-Hey fat boi!

-What's up slim Jim?

"Hey Andy what's fat and round and can't run to save his life...you?"

It did not have to be too bold and creative to let Andy know he existed to them.

He missed it.

...They were no longer pestered and many believed they had hit puberty early and were to be viewed from a distance with equal parts curiosity and observation to fuel the gossip of rumours that flow through a town eagerly awaiting stories to be told and divine information to be swilled at...

Gary came to a conclusion, hopefully the conclusion, a verdict he gladly shared with the group, "Looks as though we are off scot free then?"

"How do you make that out?"

"It's Friday, been a week and nobodies scolded us or even mentioned...the err thing that occurred..."

If they could make it to the summer holidays all would be okay?

*...and they celebrated the holidays

like any child would...*

Food! They ate a McDonalds with money swiped from their parents.

Triple cheeseburgers, large fries, Mcflurries and hot soaked in lava apple pies!

It tasted delicious and felt like freedom.

Who knew, maybe their joy was returning and their luck had been breached towards a golden fortune...?

The body had been found!!!

It was no werewolf but it did jump/fall from the first floor window the detective deduced.

It was clear the man had been battered, lived on the street a while but someone or something had inflicted brutal injuries to a compadre of the street.

"What are you on about, you idiot, something - something he says. There's a person or a group out there who did him in."

"I know, it's just that he doesn't look human, does he? Gives off vibes of the supernatural"

"Nobody can, living twenty years or more on the street. The cold malforms a man. No real food makes sure he wastes away, nobody to converse with means the mind flounders."

"Gee that's real philosophical of you man. Didn't know your mind had that peculiar bent."

Both staring at the Body found in the middle of the road that no one had reported and must have simply walked around.

"What leads humanity to such egregious ends?"

"Err I don't know but while you're on a role, why don't you think we see women on streets as much or at all really. Did he just move, I think he just twitched!"

"No, don't be stupid, the man's deader than the dodo..."

"Don't kick the body!"

"Anyway, as per your question, there's always

a man desperate enough to take a punt on a wily bint but no woman crazy enough to look for security in a man who's been out here too long. He's all bone and hair! Look at him."

"He certainly moved then did you not see it...look look he's murmuring...murmuring what...don't go near him..."

"What's he gonna do, Bite?"

The dying hairy man with broken matter for bones, when asked what happened, forced out through battered windpipes, "…three kids…"

He was taken to hospital where he later died from his injuries…

Friday night 8:55.

It did not take too long to finger the three kids who had been acting odd at school and were known to be perennial nuisances around the town.

"Yeah, they actually stopped taking the pee out of all the other kids. It was really a pleasure to teach them for once. I did wonder what was up but was having too much fun to ask," replied their teacher.

Further research found that they'd even made a gang of kids two years their senior cry whilst playing football due to how rough they were...

The rumours were now fact. It had been proven that the fall did not kill the homeless man but moreover the injuries sustained were far too vicious for a heathy man to endure let alone the sick werewolf of the street.

It was clear the children would stand trial.

Pandemo

nium

ensued!!!

The town overfilled with the joy of having something to talk about. It bonded them in an uncouth way.

"Did you…"

"I always knew they'd do something like this."

"They never were mild mannered, always used to back chat me from the age of three," said one store owner.

In coffee shops and cafe's, in bars and after dinner shows it was on the curled tip of everyones tongue.

It even hit the box upon the wall, nationwide it soared.

"Did you hear what they were saying about the boy on the television last night…how can they

The four Kid who could...

know what they're like...appear to be little bastards if you ask me."

And most people agreed.

Nobody asked who the werewolf man was though. Surely he was related to a townsperson, a distant cousin, something...

But no, there was no interest in the facts of the case. Facts make the world boring in their own way.

It was a minor celebrity of little note who mentioned, "these are only children and although all life is sacred they were only defending themselves... they hadn't even achieved the age of high school yet....How could they be seen fit to have attained the age of reason and have the sufficient motive to go around killing homeless people...it's absurd..."

His final plea (besides reminding people he had a best of album coming out), "What would ruining their lives before they have begun achieve?"

"And err also, celebrating fifty years of creating music please enjoy my latest collaboration..."

This really started the juices flowing downstream. The town hated the boys, despised the attention they received and called for harsher punishments just to be done with it.

However, the tv machine was with the youths and the slogan, "What would ruining their lives before they have begun achieve?" Was plastered everywhere.

It began to stand for everybody's childhood and children everywhere. A simple sign o' the times.

"They don't punish the kids in school why bother doing it in court. Send em to jail they'll only end up there when they're older anyway"

You could say,

Danny Croot

It began to stand for nothin at all.

The boys parents were almost glad of the flashing cameras and the sentiment they held none too dearly, "He's always been a good boy...my little darling...why it was only yesterday I remember them playing in the winter, chucking snowballs at one another...they've always been so close..."

Fo them...It was great!

Billie's mum could not possibly work at home bargains with all the cameras and sparkly lights surrounding her. They paid her to stay at home and recuperate...

Johnny's dad had more money than ever for Newcastle brown and even had the odd little cigar or ten. He just had to keep remembering things is all. Whenever a new reporter sleuthed on by, he'd pause, espouse some crap about the past, then ask for money.

And when johnny's dad got really clever he asked for the money first.

They say the scales of justice can never be tipped by public opinion but who could deny the justice of their cherubic little red faces on every talk show on all tv's across the country.

"Well we were looking for something to do…"

"We thought he was a werewolf… when he attacked Gary…we didn't know what to do."

"So he attacked you?"

"Well, he got Gary on the floor and then we saved him."

Much to Gary's chagrin the studio audience lapped it up.

Ahhhhhh, how cute.

Which was rather splendid because it was the truth after all?

It's often kinda nice in this hate infested cesspool frequently referred to as humanity for the public opinion to sway in the tide of the good and just and the righteousness swimming in the pleasant sentiment of, 'Can't we just get on with this. We are actually in this together.'

Kinda...

Before the day of the verdict, all out of hashish and Doritos and any leftover fried foods, Gary's parents revealed themselves from their smoky chambers.

Being the last to give any verdict on the predicament they were of course paid the heftiest sum.

What did they say?

"I, we do not condone what he's done… and as they keep saying… what would ruining their lives before they have begun achieve?"

It

    was

        popular

            with the times.

Call it destiny or fate or even just life's lingering line. Whatever your mind refers to it as, whichever way you discuss it, life's a most fickle mistress to tame when you've faced the scarlet red of death at such an early age.

The judge echoed these parse phrases with his own baritone voice, "Time ravages all and time rarely forgives...You'll have to live with this...they believed it was a werewolf...That abandoned building should have been boarded up or in the very least blown away...precautions were not taken and society could have done more to educate the young here today..."

So in summary, '*...what would ruining their lives before they have begun achieve?*'

*The
second
half
of the
tale
ain't half as sweet...*

As eager time ravaged faces, desolated bones and swiftly destroyed ideals…Bald! Men became bald and girls fast transformed into women of fine attitudes and gracious beauty. Soon, all too soon had their hopes slashed time and time again. It was none too fun working at home bargains or McDonalds or being somebodies (touch touchy) assistant all day. Beauty swiftly became fat, fat an angry and loose with their morals and husbands sat and watched and wished they too could materialise into something more akin to the dog they felt they always were.

Women became men, men became women and television became an all invasive fight for representation. At what cost?

The quality of television became null and void. The people had to get on with the lives and as it turned out nothing could fix what had always been broken in the first place.

In the poorest of areas teachers retired in vast quantities. They were scared of the student uprising. They were being pestered left, right and left again. The parents were worse than the children. Ill-bred and rougher than cancer at midnight.

Grocery stores and butchers were no longer in circulation, all food was purchased from a massive barn of a shop. It was cheaper and less fun this way.

Youth clubs became places for gangs to rap and chuck a basketball at each other. The streets were filled with the homeless, the mentally incapable and the downright deranged…

There were too many people and not enough things to do. Nobody wanted to work and those who did, soon gave it up when benefits could prove far more profitable…and less effort.

Immigration became a problem and they too, worked for a bit then found it far easier, not knowing the language, to just sit on benefits and abuse each other over bottles of caramel covered alcoholic whisky knock off's from the local barn of a supermarket.

Some people and couples made it out of the towns and the cities and lived off of the grid doing none too much with the night!

Others held parties and get togethers and watched as their friends moved further away and that six o' clock aperitif became a morning livener oh too easily and oh so swiftly...

Drinking the day away, far away from the populace was a dream for many and a nightmare for those who did not know they were living it.

Some, did in fact became rich and achieved what they thought they wanted to achieve in this world and then wondered why they felt empty, alienated and lonesome in a mansion surrounded by a smily-smily family they never saw and acquaintances they knew all too well.

Some women went insane from too much love, not enough love, never the right amount of love.

Time rolls on as everyone else rolls the dice…

Even the leaders spoke like morons with webbed toes for tongues. Agendas were rife and all too overt. It was little one could do but survive and avoid. Avoid and survive.

The place had no culture to lift oneself up within.

Rarely did one read. Rarely did one watch a movie from a year that wasn't released in the one they were in. Rarely did one listen to another human being and ponder upon the implications of what they truly meant.

Why were the wet eyes so sad...yet the story was of her pinky finger?

Where were the gods of yesteryears? The divine people who could do no wrong… Who were real and shiny and phosphorescent in personality…

Well, they were cancelled, yet to make a comeback in a world where disenchantment was the norm and there was no compassion lost for the things that grown up kids (adults) said.

The old were replaced by the young and each knew they knew better than what had gone on before. Yet nothin really changed. Music had gotten worse, or the best most people could suggest was, "Music is different now, most different."

There's an outpouring of hate on all facets of the media, "What's changed." They say whilst scoffing a stale bagel and a milky cup of coffee froth.

"Yeah, I know tell me about it, celebrity this, pile of shite celebrity that again and again and again, when's the working man gonna be represented."

Nobody told them Emile Zola had been doing

this nearly two hundred years ago.

Why, was the working man rarely represented?

Boring, his work, his state of being was phenomenally and excruciatingly boring.

Even when he, Zola, added sex to sell, it was most terribly, like adhesive stuck to the back of your head, stifling.

...yet life meanders on and there is no room for improvement for the three friends whose lives went nowhere...even if they did stray a little into success or newness, it did not last long enough to savour the lessening of life's anhedonic taste...

Life, the name of the hazy game we all play, life and chaos and love are full of the fatally ripe last breaths that will connivingly, almost invisibly have its fondling way with us all...there really is no escape.

Johnny's dad, right before he died, was living a bit of a wobbly. He couldn't help but repeat, "Life is Boredom with the odd surprise in the gall bladder."

He had brain cancer and had been on a drunken cruise of a bender for nearly a decade.

He'd wobble around the streets repeating his impromptu manifesto for all who would never hear, "Life is Boredom with the odd surprise in the gall bladder."

He really began to stress the is every time he said it. Oftentimes the later it got, so late in fact, it would pretty much be early for anybody else, repeatin like a one note flute, "is is is is is is is is."

No woman had touched him and the older he got, the less he could see what was right infront of his face… his final words to Johnny, 'It truly was and is most important to do nothing at all. That way, they can't get ya.'

If those words, the sentiment even, were not taken to heart... it's because they were already there, embedded like a surreptitious soul inside a snake, hiding a jewel, the snake did not know the value of.

Perennially in the air, felt on the inside and on the out.

As for Billy...

Rumour has it Billy turned towards being a drifter of sorts, a wondering nomad if you will. He failed at that. He never made it too far. Could always be found hanging around woods about a mile away from the town or lingering along the canals and rivers no further than a stroll away.

The towns tittle tattle on the street, often said and received with composed nonchalance was, "Billy had last been seen pedalling peacefully a stolen kids bike along the motorway."

They would not have been surprised if the gravity of a sixteen wheeler took him out of this world.

In fact it would have done them a favour, for his sadness, a child with such a bombastic nature, such winsome innocence begged at them to think no more at what had been lost…

If there was a funeral for Billy, nobody attended.

Even the people full of the caffeine of coffee bean rhetoric had better stuff to complain about, "I'm pretty sure they've changed the flavour of bread. Here taste it...it-it's off-"

"Its got granary seeds on it ya fool!"

"I tell you its always looked like this and it's never tasted worse. Bah," spits it out. "It's all oniony"

Billy had been defeated and crushed long before the gravity of a sixteen wheeler took him out of this world.

What became of the, other,

likely lads?

It was not until a chance encounter in a bar, low lit, poor, real piss poor customer service, where all the spirits are served with coke, whether asked for or not... Gary sat down for a bit of peace and at least the verisimilitude of quiet.

It was no high school reunion that had brought him back to town but more death and more drudgery. Gary's parents had split and his mother was slowly dying, of what, nobody knew.

She complained and complained of her life, suddenly unloved, every regret she held in her head, never been loved, never done anything worthwhile, struggled to get a job, couldn't hold down a job, of how she had misspent her years with her son, even the liquor would not stay down, she could not sleep, she was unloved and had lived all wrong for most of the life she could recall...

It was his parents joint paranoia that forced Gary to make a little out of himself. Surprising, the sheer velocity with which he finished school and fucked off to the nearest city and took any job given to him...

"Heard from Billy anytime in last twenty years?" A cold voice said.

"I ave no change, fuck off will ya, trying to search for a little-"

"Don't you know who I...look at me...Gary buddy it's been."

Gary gave him the once over and although Gary had aged, he'd kept in shape, ate little, fasted in-between running and work. He could not recognise this fatso before him for a lifetime of solid cashflow.

"It's me, Johnny!" He attempted a smile full of gravitas.

"Get fucked. There's no way, no way...fat Andy more like...what happened...you, you...you Might *as well sit down and I'll order you the cheapest drink possible then eh?"*

...You cannot recapture, perhaps, what once was never there...

Johnny worked at Home Bargains.

Johnny talks a lot.

Johnny talked around the marrow of the twenty-first century disease.

Gary drank.

Johnny laughs at how he really did work at home bargains. He had one shift, not so long ago, in a supervisory role at Superdrug for about a week, "…Caught stealing."

"Cigarettes?" *Gary replied to show he was still listening.*

"No time, I stole time. Stayed at home…couldn't bring myself to go in, hated it and actually missed home bargains. I ended up back there within the week…they're always hiring."

They wondered into talking about the other facets of life, of women, of events, of people they once knew, teachers and the hometown…nothing too deep or of note.

Johnny matched Gary drink for drink. Giving his old pal a kind ear all the way... he would have liked to disappear into a void. An unknown collapsed refuge in time that differed to death. Life clings weirdly to a man when he hits a certain age, he wears it differently depending on the choices he's made and what's been thrust at him.

No, this void would be a subtle peace smothered in oceans calm.

If it were not for Gary...

"So what do you do Gary?"

"Nothin…"

"Well I've been contemplating… you listening, here here, Gary-Gary…Gary…"

"Yes, I'm listening."

"Well…I've been thinking long and hard…"

"Do not say it," bluntly Gary replied, *"do not even think it…"*

Gary repeated the sentiment twice fold. Eyes flashed and nostrils flared.

Johnny took note, for now…

It took five drinks.

It took seven drinks.

It lead to downing spirits of a higher percent in alcohol (after shoving the bartender away from the dirty keg of coke he kept underneath the desk that is).

The night was calm and summer was fast encroaching upon the stillness of the town where they had watched their childhood blossom... before this hasty desolation had ensnared them.

"Dirty pizza or kebab?"

Gary did not answer, it was all he could do, to nod laconically to his old friend.

"You turned out alright didn't you? You look good, smell kinda clean and have most of your hair..."

"There's no way that's correct."

"See, now it's you what talks like a teacher?"

"I was once..."

In an effort to chase the lost yesterdays of youth

Gary relented…

"I got fired for one complaint..."

"Which was, come on, I need this..."

"What a thing to say..."

"It's the truth, I haven't had a friend..."

Garys eyes flared this time and his nostrils damn near popped off of his face.

"Was this pupil of yours at least hot? Was she one of the hotties? I remember in our class-"

"No, don't be disgusting, the idea of a teenager is sexy, actually looking at them and hearing them talk... They're children, barely formed an thicker than bases of the old oak tree we used to relax beneath...how did you know I was a teacher?"

"You smell like one."

"Re-ally?"

"No, everybody roun ere knows everything about everyone…Did you?"

"Did I what?"

"Was the complaint genuine?"

"If I told you she stunk and had clammy pits reminiscent of Rebecca Jones you'd get the picture… all I did was to try and nurture her literary talent so she did not undertake the suicidal option."

"What about the mum and dad?"

"I had a word with them about their daughters inappropriate behaviour…"

"And?"

"They were even mankier and confused than she was."

"Who put in the complaint, how did you get caught?"

"Kids, kids made up a stupid little rhyme that spread around the school and surrounding areas like wild fires of Babylon..."

...The streets were alive with teens who had come of age, engagement parties, fancy dress ups and a flood of pissing in the alleys gave the night the feel of alive...

"Would it be wrong to ask what the rhyme was?"

"Fuck yes, now what are you having?"

"Both…I'd like a dirty bastard pizza and a kebab?"

"You'll end up like fat Andy."

"Fat Andy lost all his weight."

"No way!"

"His misses on the other hand…elephant sized would be a minor compliment."

They ate their food on a soggy bench, away from the movement, away from the alive...

"Nothing in life... is worth doing in this life... is it?" Gary said in-between bites of slop and various meat combinations.

"You think there's another life?"

"No... that's not what I meant."

"Hey my life's been abject misery..." Gary knew it was coming, he was too relaxed now, too drunk to reach out and slap his old friends words away,"... ever since that night?"

He stood up, "Let's go back there right now!"

"No way."

"Conquer our demons."

"That doesn't really mean anything does it? Conquer our demons pah!"

"Maybe we'll have unsurmountable fortune, or maybe your dad really was right and nobody amounts to anything around here. What can be the harm?"

"It's not that…"

"Good, leave it there then, might shut you up for a while…"

And ladies and gentlemen of the jury, they entered that still somehow abandoned wreckage of a building. Still, the signs had not been replaced in fifteen years and nobody had done anything about the eye sore that was, shall we say, the shoddier *part of town.*

I ask you...

What happened to the kids who could never age?

The kids who could do no wrong and got away scot free last time around?

Was it really their fault they were attacked once more whilst trying to salvage the ruins of their lives? The hairy man or werewolf shall we say bust Gary's shoulder and nearly bit Johnny's ear off. He's currently missing the tip of his little pinky finger aren't ya?

Johnny nodded.

Gary turned away from their lawyer. He knew what was coming...

"The only reason, well boys... would you like to say why you did not beat him earlier and why you have bruises, slashes by the dozen and a broken collarbone... Come on speak up. It was two on one after all, wasn't it....Gary...Johnny you're not kids anymore you're going to have to answer at some point."

Pause.

They held back tears and whatever else was clogging they hearts and minds, "It was Billy."

"Thank you, aha, how could these boys know it was their once triumphant friend? Quite simply, they could not...but with the aid of the coroners report it can be stated with forthright fact that it was indeed Billy."

"It just had to be."

The jury appeared unmoved. As if death was in fact death. None of the jurors lived in the town. Perhaps none of them knew anything at all about its rich historical tapestry...

In order to stop the slight commotion that was beginning to gyrate, the judge added, "Jurors must be reminded murder is murder, doesn't matter who-"

"Yes, but it does matter how?" Their lawyer replied.

"I'd like to paint you a picture if you shall allow-"

"Please no more, you've talked enough, your overly loquacious tongue and elegant whims have informed us all enough."

The jurors breathed a hefty sigh of relief.

"Thank you for your kind words, if I may, I

shall leave you with this final conundrum..."

"NO MORE PLEASE!"

"Can kids who were let off in the prime of their life be held accountable for the same crime now... and if so, why?"

The jurors retreated to the closed off room in order to make their verdict.

They were most torn. Hungry, tired and torn.

"But they were drunk, older and should have known better."

"Why even go back the old buildings. Surely they're old enough..."

"What shitty lives they all lead round ere?"

"That's not an issue."

"Yes it is. Either it's all relevant or nothing is."

"I'm tired, just pick one and i'll agree. I wanna go home."

The only facet of the case they all mimicked in one way or another was:

"Why let them off as children... when did they stop being youths and why was it so easy to

condemn an adult who looked...rough to say the least...but never the same children...the children that are these ragged men before us..."

"Now you're starting to sound like that god damn lawyer."

"Tis a phenomenon..."

"Hey, if we condemn them right now, maybe their lives will be even better in the prison system."

The verdict was a struggle.

It was too hard of a moral quandary.

It went on for days…

It was only when the same faded minor celebrity of no note came to the media's attention and said, "I was wrong, you can let kids off but these guys should have known better. They must have been rotten from the start. If they'd been condemned their friend would still be alive....After he'd been let out of care of course...err...hmmm...Don't forget my latest best of cd. It's the best of the best of's, as well as some rarities not on the last four best of's..."

Now the societal ruckus had calmed down, the jurors could think straight and finally deliver that fatal verdict...

However the verdict became obscured and was not as widely known because...

...Around the same time a world famous superstar of a celebrity had been in abusive relationship with a female actress and apparently this trumped all news outlets, all wars, all beauty products that steamed the face into a red oblivion.

It was everywhere and continued for quite some time.

Twas rather juicy...

However...

There was and is a time when kids were free... *and* **adults** *also...*

As for Billy and Johnny and Gary?

Who cares?

Nobody else did.

www.ingramcontent.com/pod-product-compliance
Lightning Source LLC
Chambersburg PA
CBHW052154220526
45471CB00004B/1673